D1105857

Pennsylvania

Jill Wheeler

Visit us at
www.abdopublishing.com

Published by ABDO Publishing Company, 8000 West 78th Street, Suite 310, Edina, Minnesota 55439 USA. Copyright ©2010 by Abdo Consulting Group, Inc. International copyrights reserved in all countries. No part of this book may be reproduced in any form without written permission from the publisher. The Checkerboard Library™ is a trademark and logo of ABDO Publishing Company.

Printed in the United States.

Editor: John Hamilton
Graphic Design: Sue Hamilton
Cover Illustration: Neil Klinepier
Cover Photo: iStock Photo

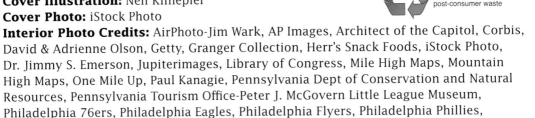

Interior Photo Credits: AirPhoto-Jim Wark, AP Images, Architect of the Capitol, Corbis, David & Adrienne Olson, Getty, Granger Collection, Herr's Snack Foods, iStock Photo, Dr. Jimmy S. Emerson, Jupiterimages, Library of Congress, Mile High Maps, Mountain High Maps, One Mile Up, Paul Kanagie, Pennsylvania Dept of Conservation and Natural Resources, Pennsylvania Tourism Office-Peter J. McGovern Little League Museum, Philadelphia 76ers, Philadelphia Eagles, Philadelphia Flyers, Philadelphia Phillies, Pioneer Tunnel Coal Mine, Pittsburgh Penguins, Pittsburgh Pirates, Pittsburgh Steelers.
Statistics: State population statistics taken from 2008 U.S. Census Bureau estimates. City and town population statistics taken from July 1, 2007, U.S. Census Bureau estimates. Land and water area statistics taken from 2000 Census, U.S. Census Bureau.

Library of Congress Cataloging-in-Publication Data

Wheeler, Jill C., 1964-
  Pennsylvania / Jill C. Wheeler.
      p. cm. -- (The United States)
  Includes index.
  ISBN 978-1-60453-673-7
  1. Pennsylvania--Juvenile literature. I. Title.
  F149.3.W48 2010
  974.8--dc22
                          2008052397

Table of Contents

The Keystone State

Pennsylvania is a beautiful state with an important history. It is called the Keystone State because of its central location in the original 13 American colonies. Our country's first government met in Pennsylvania. This government was called the Continental Congress. Philadelphia, Pennsylvania, was the capital of the United States during the country's early years. The Declaration of Independence was signed in Pennsylvania. Also, the Liberty Bell is in Pennsylvania. It was an important symbol of freedom during the Revolutionary War.

Pennsylvania also has important sports teams, museums, and entertainment. The state is considered the chocolate capital of the world. There is always something to do in the Keystone State.

At Pennsylvania's Washington Crossing, Revolutionary War actors march to re-enact George Washington's Christmas crossing of the Delaware River in 1776.

Quick Facts

Name: Pennsylvania means "Penn's Woods." The state was named in honor of English Admiral Sir William Penn, the father of the colony's founder, William Penn.

State Capital: Harrisburg, population 47,196

Date of Statehood: December 12, 1787 (2nd state)

Population: 12,448,279 (6th-most populous state)

Area (Total Land and Water): 46,055 square miles (119,282 sq km), 33rd-largest state

Largest City: Philadelphia, population 1,449,634

Nickname: The Keystone State

Motto: Virtue, Liberty, and Independence

State Bird: Ruffed Grouse

Trilobyte

Mt. Davis

Delaware River

James Buchanan

State Flower: Mountain Laurel

State Fossil: *Phacops rana* (trilobyte)

State Tree: Hemlock

State Song: "Pennsylvania"

Highest Point: 3,213 feet (979 m), Mount Davis

Lowest Point: 0 feet (0 m), Delaware River

Average July Temperature: 71°F (22°C)

Record High Temperature: 111°F (44°C) in Phoenixville, July 10, 1936

Average January Temperature: 27°F (-3°C)

Record Low Temperature: -42°F (-41°C) in Smethport, January 5, 1904

Average Annual Precipitation: 41 inches (104 cm)

Number of U.S. Senators: 2

Number of U.S. Representatives: 19

U.S. Presidents Born in Pennsylvania: James Buchanan (1857-1861)

U.S. Postal Service Abbreviation: PA

Geography

Pennsylvania is in the northeast United States in a region called the Middle Atlantic. It borders Delaware and Maryland to the south, and West Virginia to the southwest. Ohio is to the west. New York is north of Pennsylvania, and New Jersey is to the east.

There are three major rivers in Pennsylvania. The Delaware River makes up the southeast border of the state. The Ohio River is in western Pennsylvania. The Susquehanna River is in the center of the state. The largest natural lake in Pennsylvania is Conneaut Lake.

Lake Erie is in the northwest corner of Pennsylvania. It is one of the five Great Lakes. The northwest corner of Pennsylvania is called the Great Lakes Plain. It is made up of mostly flat land.

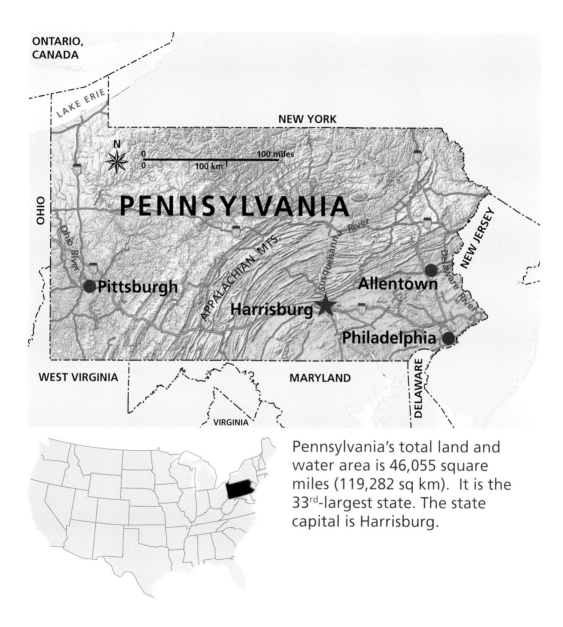

Pennsylvania's total land and water area is 46,055 square miles (119,282 sq km). It is the 33rd-largest state. The state capital is Harrisburg.

Next to the Great Lakes Plain is the High Plateau region. This region is called the Appalachian or Allegheny Plateau. These are flat-topped mountains. They cover the northwest part of the state. There are very few people in this region. There is a lot of coal and oil. The High Plateau region gets taller and more rugged as it becomes a part of the Appalachian Mountains.

Rugged mountains drop to forested rolling hills in Pennsylvania.

Good soil has made for many excellent farms in the eastern part of Pennsylvania.

Moving east from the Appalachian Mountains the land gets flatter. It becomes level at the Piedmont Plateau. There are rolling hills and fertile soil in this area of Pennsylvania.

In the southeast corner is the Atlantic Coastal Plain. This is a very flat and fertile area and is similar to the Great Lakes Plain.

Climate and Weather

Mist from a power washer cools off a boy during a summer heat wave.

Pennsylvania has four distinct seasons. The northwest part of the state is colder and snowier. The southeast is warmer and more humid. The average winter temperature is 30 degrees Fahrenheit (-1°C). In spring, the weather gets warmer and rainy. The summer temperature is usually 60 to 70 degrees Fahrenheit (16°C to 21°C). Summers tend to be very humid. In the fall, temperatures drop very quickly. The leaves on the trees change color and are very beautiful.

Another important part of Pennsylvania's weather is the presence of acid rain. The state has more heavily polluted and acidic rain than almost anywhere else in the United States. This rain kills fish. It also can get into drinking water and make people sick. Pennsylvanians are working to correct the damage done by acid rain.

With the coal-fired Bruce Mansfield Power Plant operating nearby, a man looks at the effects of acid rain on playground equipment in a nearby, and rarely used, park in Shippingport, Pennsylvania.

Plants and Animals

Pennsylvania has almost 400 species of birds. Some birds native to Pennsylvania include ruffed grouse, wild turkeys, bobwhite quail, Canada geese, screech owls, mallard ducks, great blue herons, plus many songbirds.

Other creatures in Pennsylvania forests include black bears, white-tailed deer, rabbits, black and gray squirrels, raccoons, beavers, foxes, and mink. In addition, there are frogs, salamanders, opossums, skunks, woodchucks, wildcats and Indiana bats. The largest animal in Pennsylvania is the elk.

The Indiana bat is an endangered species. Abandoned mines have become a place where bats are finding new homes.

Elk roam the forests of Pennsylvania.

Black Bear

Spotted Salamander

Great Blue Heron

Some fish native to Pennsylvania's rivers and lakes are bass, catfish, sunfish, northern pike, walleye, bluegill, muskellunge, and black crappie. There also are many harmless snakes and three poisonous species of snakes. These poisonous snakes are the copperhead, timber rattlesnake, and Eastern Massasauga rattlesnake. There are many species of turtles in Pennsylvania, including the wood, map, Eastern box and bog turtles.

Gray Treefrog

Black Rat Snake

Map Turtle

About three-fifths of Pennsylvania is forest. Trees found in the High Plateau region include beech, hemlock, and maple trees. In the south, there are ash, aspen, cherry, hickory, birch, oak, poplar, sycamore, walnut, and red and yellow maple trees. There are also blackberry, raspberry, and elderberry bushes in the mountains of Pennsylvania.

Many flowers grow throughout the state. There are azaleas, rhododendrons, and honeysuckles. Mountain laurels are the state flower of Pennsylvania. They grow in many places.

Blackberries

Raspberries

Elderberries

History

Native American tribes in Pennsylvania included the Susquehannock, the Iroquois, the Lenni Lenape, and the Shawnee. Some of these people lived in Pennsylvania 16,000 years ago.

John Smith

In 1608, Englishman John Smith became the first European to visit the Pennsylvania area. In 1609, English explorer Henry Hudson followed. He was working for the Dutch. He claimed the Pennsylvania area for his employer.

The Dutch held the Pennsylvania area for many years. However, Sweden also started settlements, and a fight broke out over who should own the land. The Dutch won that fight, only to lose the land to England in 1664.

After setting up his colony in Pennsylvania in 1861, William Penn traded goods and established treaties with local Native Americans.

England's King Charles II gave Pennsylvania to William Penn in 1681. Penn was a Quaker. He wanted his new territory to be a place where all religions were allowed. As governor, Penn wrote a state constitution called the *Frame of Government*. This document gave people who lived in Pennsylvania the right to own land. They also were granted other freedoms.

Carpenters' Hall in Philadelphia, Pennsylvania, was the meeting place of the First Continental Congress in 1774.

In 1774, the First Continental Congress met in Philadelphia, Pennsylvania. They were representatives of the people of the American colonies. They talked about their frustrations with the British government. In 1776, they signed the Declaration of Independence. It was a vote for independence from Great Britain.

Philadelphia served as the capital of the new nation for several years before it was moved to Washington, D.C., in 1800. Pennsylvania became the second state in the Union after ratifying the Constitution in 1787. Pennsylvania continued to play an important role in helping the new country. The state manufactured many goods that the nation's people needed.

George Washington led the Constitutional Convention in Philadelphia in 1787. After ratifying the Constitution, Pennsylvania became the second state in the Union.

A soldier holds the tattered remains of the Eighth Pennsylvania Infantry Regiment. Some of the Civil War's bloodiest battles occurred in Pennsylvania.

During the early- and mid-1800s, many African American slaves from Southern states fled to Pennsylvania. In fact, many Pennsylvanians tried to make the United States safe for African Americans. More than 400,000 soldiers from the state fought in the Union Army during the Civil War (1861-1865).

A steel and a coal plant in Pennsylvania in 1905.

In the late 1800s, Pennsylvania became a powerful manufacturing center. The state had many natural resources, including coal and lumber. It was a leader in iron and steel production. Mills, foundries, railroads, and shipyards sprang up. During World War I and World War II, Pennsylvania gave troops, steel, coal, and ships to the war effort.

In the 1960s until the mid-1980s, Pennsylvania suffered an economic decline. It became known as part of the "rust belt." Competition from foreign countries greatly hurt heavy industries like steel and machinery manufacturing. To bring its economy back, Pennsylvania in recent years has diversified. It now relies more and more on high-technology industries, plus companies in the service sector, like health care, finance, and insurance.

Did You Know?

- The Pioneer Tunnel in Ashland leads into a coal mine. The mine closed in 1931. There is a train that goes 1,800 feet (549 m) into the earth. Visitors can learn how coal was mined.

- Each autumn, more than 18,000 birds of prey fly over the Hawk Mountain Sanctuary northeast of Harrisburg.

- Williamsport is a town in central Pennsylvania where Little League Baseball began. The Peter J. McGovern Little League Baseball Museum is in South Williamsport.

Each year South Williamsport also hosts the Little League Baseball World Series.

- Pennsylvania has a state fossil. Some students were studying about a species of trilobite called *Phacops rana*. It was a small, ancient sea animal. The students wrote to the state government and asked that *Phacops rana* be made the state fossil. It did on December 5, 1988.

- There was a major nuclear accident in Pennsylvania in 1979. It happened near Harrisburg on an island called Three Mile Island. A nuclear power plant overheated and contaminated the air. Thousands of people fled the area as a precaution.

People

Will Smith (1968-) began performing rap at the age of 12. During the 1980s and early 1990s, he became a music superstar before turning to acting. Smith has been in such hits as *Independence Day*, *I, Robot*, *Men In Black*, and other blockbusters. He has been nominated for and won many awards. Smith was born in Philadelphia.

Milton Hershey (1857-1945) opened the Hershey Chocolate Company in 1894. Today the company is world famous for chocolate bars and kisses. Milton Hershey was born in a small town called Derry Church. That town is now called Hershey because of the huge chocolate factory there.

The Hershey Chocolate Factory

Arnold Palmer (1929-) is a golf legend. He was the first four-time winner of The Masters, a golf championship. He also was the first golfer to win $1 million in prize money. Palmer was born in Latrobe.

Reggie Jackson (1946-) played for the New York Yankees and Oakland A's Major League Baseball teams in the 1960s through the 1980s. He is the sixth-leading home run hitter. Jackson helped the Yankees win two World Series championships. He was inducted into the Baseball Hall of Fame in 1993. Jackson was born in Wyncote.

Daniel Hale Williams (1856-1931) performed the first successful heart surgery. He was an African American who founded Provident Hospital, the first hospital to accept patients regardless of race. It also was the first hospital to have African Americans on staff. Williams was born in Hollidaysburg, Pennsylvania.

Taylor Swift (1989-) is an award-winning singer-songwriter. Swift released her first professional album in 2006, which went to the top of the country music charts. She has won several country music awards, including Album of the Year in 2009 for *Fearless*. Swift was born in Wyomissing.

Cities

Philadelphia is the biggest city in Pennsylvania. Its population is 1,449,634. Independence National Historical Park is where the Declaration of Independence was signed. The Liberty Bell is housed there. At the Academy of Natural Sciences, museum visitors can see a fully animated dinosaur. The University of Pennsylvania also is located in Philadelphia.

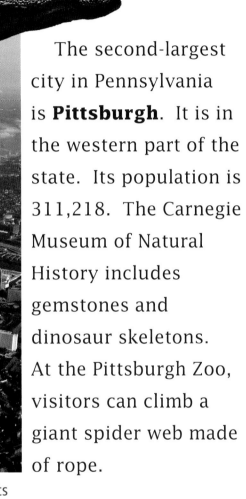

The second-largest city in Pennsylvania is **Pittsburgh**. It is in the western part of the state. Its population is 311,218. The Carnegie Museum of Natural History includes gemstones and dinosaur skeletons. At the Pittsburgh Zoo, visitors can climb a giant spider web made of rope.

A huge dinosaur statue greets visitors to the Carnegie Museum of Natural History.

The capital of Pennsylvania is **Harrisburg**. Its population is about 47,196. The city is located in south-central Pennsylvania, in a fertile agricultural area called the Susquehanna Valley. The Pennsylvania Farm Show is one of the largest farm fairs in the country. Many people also visit the Whitaker Center for Science and the Arts.

The city of **Allentown** has a population of about 107,117. It is located in eastern Pennsylvania, north of Philadelphia. Many large companies have their headquarters in Allentown, including Mack Trucks, a leading truck manufacturer.

Transportation

Philadelphia was Pennsylvania's first major port. Goods could be shipped down the Delaware River to the Atlantic Ocean. Goods also could be transported to

Pennsylvania coal is transported by ship and by train.

and from Pennsylvania by Lake Erie. Today, the Port of Pittsburgh is one of the nation's busiest inland ports.

Construction of the Philadelphia-Lancaster Turnpike was completed in 1794. It was the first major hard-surface road in America. It was 62 miles (98 km) long.

The first modern highway was in Pennsylvania, too. It opened to the public in 1940. Today, there are about 120,000 miles (193,121 km) of highways in the state.

In 1850, railroads were first built across the Appalachian Mountains in Pennsylvania. Today, there are more than 5,100 miles (8,208 km) of railways in the state, which ranks fifth in the nation.

The Blue Mountain Tunnel is one of seven tunnels created for the Pennsylvania Turnpike. It is 4,339 feet (1,323 m) long.

Natural Resources

More than a fourth of Pennsylvania is farmland. There are about 58,000 farms in the state. Pennsylvania produces 59 percent of the country's mushrooms each year. Pennsylvania produces many other crops as well, including wheat, apples, corn, hay, soybeans, oats, and potatoes. In southern Pennsylvania, tomatoes, grapes, peaches, and strawberries also are grown.

Pennsylvania farmers raise cattle, hogs, and chickens. The state is the fifth-largest producer of milk in the United States. Pennsylvania farmers also produce eggs and grow greenhouse and nursery products.

Pennsylvania is the fifth-largest producer of milk in the United States.

Coal accounts for most of Pennsylvania's mineral wealth. The mining of coal, iron, and oil were once a big part of the state's economy, but their importance has dropped in recent years. Iron, limestone, natural gas, oil, sand, and gravel continue to be mined in Pennsylvania today.

A coal miner knocks down a wall at an underground mine in western Pennsylvania. There are also many surface strip mines in the state.

Industry

Service industries are very important to Pennsylvania today. Such jobs include banking, health care, tourism, and retail trade. The other part of the population is mainly involved in industry. These people typically work in factories and manufacture goods that people buy.

Pennsylvania factories produce clothes, glass, machinery, printed materials, steel, electronics, and transportation equipment. They also make chemicals such as paint and medicine. Food is an important product of Pennsylvania, too. More snack foods are made in Pennsylvania than in any other part of the United States.

Herr's snack foods are made in Nottingham, Pennsylvania.

Many people come to visit Independence Hall in Philadelphia, Pennsylvania. It is where the Declaration of Independence and the U.S. Constitution were signed. People also come to see the Liberty Bell. It once was in Independence Hall's bell tower, but now is across the street in the Liberty Bell Center.

Sports

There are many popular sports teams in Pennsylvania. The Philadelphia Phillies and the Pittsburgh Pirates

are Major League Baseball teams. The Philadelphia 76ers are members of the National Basketball Association.

Pennsylvania's two National Football League teams include the Pittsburgh

Steelers and the Philadelphia Eagles. The state's National Hockey League

teams are the Pittsburgh Penguins and the Philadelphia Flyers. South Williamsport's yearly Little League

Baseball World Series is another big sporting attraction.

Pennsylvania is also known for its outdoor activities. Whitewater rafting, canoeing, hiking, backpacking, fishing, and skiing are all popular sports. With its beautiful hills and wilderness, it's no wonder so many Pennsylvanians love to spend their time outdoors.

A kayaker on the Youghiogheny River at Ohiopyle State Park. Some of the best whitewater kayaking and rafting in the eastern United States is on this river, which is south of Pittsburgh, Pennsylvania.

Entertainment

Pennsylvania is full of interesting things to do. You can visit Punxsutawney Phil and see the famous, weather-predicting groundhog. The Carnegie Science Center in Pittsburgh is a famous hand-on museum.

Punxsutawney Phil comes out of his burrow every February 2 in Punxsutawney, Pennsylvania. If he sees his shadow, legend says there will be six more weeks of winter.

There is also Titusville's Drake Well Museum, the Johnstown Flood Museum, and the State Museum of Pennsylvania in Harrisburg. Northwest of Philadelphia, visitors can see George Washington's headquarters at Valley Forge National Historical Park.

The Lenni Lenape tribe of Native Americans hosts an annual Corn Festival in Allentown. There also is a festival in which participants reenact the major Civil War battle fought at Gettysburg.

At Hershey Park in Hershey, Pennsylvania, there is a chocolate-making tour and free samples of the company's world-famous candy. There is also an amusement park.

Many people come to Hershey, Pennsylvania, to enjoy the Hershey's Chocolate World amusement park.

Timeline

1609—Henry Hudson claims the Pennsylvania area for his Dutch employers.

1643—The Swedes begin Pennsylvania's first permanent European settlement.

1664—England gains control of the Pennsylvania area.

1681—England's King Charles II gives Pennsylvania to William Penn.

1774—The First Continental Congress meets in Philadelphia.

1776—The Declaration of Independence is signed in Philadelphia.

1787—Pennsylvania becomes the second state to ratify the U.S. Constitution.

1794—The first major hard-surface road opens between Philadelphia and Lancaster.

1859—The nation's first successful oil well is constructed near Titusville.

1979—Three Mile Island nuclear power plant accident occurs.

2009—Pittsburgh Steelers win the Super Bowl for the sixth time.

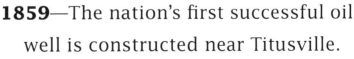

Glossary

Acid Rain—Rain that becomes slightly acid because of air pollution, especially from coal-burning power plants. Acid rain hurts forests and lakes.

Birds of Prey—Birds that hunt smaller birds, as well as small mammals and rodents like mice and chipmunks.

Choreographer—A person who creates and arranges dance movements and patterns.

Coal—A fossil fuel that currently provides about half of the country's electricity.

Constitution—A set of laws that establish the rules and principles of a country or organization.

Contaminate—To pollute.

Continental Congress—The government assembled by the 13 American colonies when they revolted against British rule.

Fossil—The preserved remains or impression of prehistoric animals or plants in stone.

Plateau—A relatively flat area of high ground.

Quaker—A member of the Religious Society of Friends. The Quakers are a Christian movement founded in 1650 by George Fox. They believe in principles of peace and tolerance.

Service Industry—Businesses that do work for customers, like insurance or health care. Service industries do not normally manufacture things.

Territory—A piece of land that is under the control of a country or ruler.

Index

PENNSYLVANIA